CW00347397

Nita Mehta's

TANDOORI
COOKING in the OVEN

Vegetarian

Nita Mehta

B.Sc. (Home Science), M.Sc. (Food and Nutrition), Gold Medalist

TANYA MEHTA

SNAB
Excellence in Books

TANDOORI
COOKING in the OVEN

SNAB
Excellence in Books

Snab Publishers Pvt Ltd

Corporate Office
3A/3, Asaf Ali Road, New Delhi 110 002
Phone: +91 11 2325 2948, 2325 0091
Telefax: +91 11 2325 0091
E-mail: nitamehta@nitamehta.com
Website: www.nitamehta.com

ISBN 978-81-7869-038-4

7th Print 2012

Printed at HT Media Ltd., Noida

Contributing Writers:
Anurag Mehta
Tanya Mehta
Subhash Mehta

Editors :
Sangeeta
Sunita

Distributed by :
NITA MEHTA BOOKS
3A/3, Asaf Ali Road, New Delhi - 02

Distribution Centre :
D16/1, Okhla Industrial Area, Phase-I,
New Delhi - 110020
Tel.: 26813199, 26813200
E-mail: nitamehta.mehta@gmail.com

Editorial and Marketing office
E-159, Greater Kailash II, New Delhi 110 048

Food Styling and Photography by Snab
Typesetting by National Information Technology Academy
3A/3, Asaf Ali Road, New Delhi 110 002

Recipe Development & Testing:
Nita Mehta Foods - R & D Centre
3A/3, Asaf Ali Road, New Delhi - 110002
E-143, Amar Colony, Lajpat Nagar-IV, New Delhi - 110024

Price: Rs. 89/-

Introduction

Offer your loved ones tandoori food from your kitchen even if you do not have a conventional clay tandoor. Mouth watering tikkas and succulent kebabs can be on the table, fresh from the Oven. No more buying ready made ones! A gas tandoor can also be used very successfully instead of the oven or the conventional clay tandoor.

Tandoori food is generally low in calories and simple to prepare, although it looks amazing on the table. Good for family meals as well as entertaining. There are some special tikkas/kebabs for parties or special occasions like *Saunfiya Paneer tikka, Malai khumb, Tandoori kathal* etc. which are sure to be a hit at any party. Some delicious pan fried kebabs and seekhs like *matar makhana kebab and bhutte ke seekh* are also included in the book.

Breads, chutneys and other accompaniments of a tandoori meal too are given to make the book complete. Serve kebabs from this book as snacks or transform tikkas to meal time masala dishes like *tandoori paneer ki subzi, Exotic barbecue platter* etc. Enjoy!

Nita Mehta

Contents

Tikkas   11

Indian Breads

Chutneys & Salads   92

Accompaniments   97

Tips for perfect tandoori cooking (barbecuing)...

- Tandoori food should be barbecued on the grill rack or wire rack (*jaali*) of the oven and not on the oven tray. When the food is put on the tray, the liquid that drips keeps collecting around the food. This does not let the food get crisp on the outside. When it is on the wire rack, the liquid drips down. These drippings can be collected on a tray covered with aluminium foil and placed under the rack.
- Cut the pieces of food according to the space in between the wires of the grill. If the distance between the wires of the rack is too wide, and there is a chance of your piece slipping, then cover the wire rack with a well greased **aluminium foil**.
- The size of tikkas should not be **too small**. After getting cooked they shrink. A very small piece after getting cooked can turn hard.
- While skewering or placing pieces of vegetables, the pieces should be arranged such that there is atleast **1" gap** between them so that each piece can get it's own space and heat all around to get cooked properly.
- When skewering vegetables, it is advisable to use **thinner skewers**, then there is less chance of the vegetable to break.

TIKKAS

Achaari Paneer Tikka

Pickle flavoured masala paneer tikka.

Picture on cover   *Makes 10-12*

400 gms paneer - cut into 1½" rectangles of ¾-1" thickness
2 tsp ginger-garlic paste
1 tsp cornflour
1 cup curd - hang in a muslin cloth for ½ hour
2 tbsp oil
½ tsp haldi (turmeric) powder
1 tsp amchoor (dried mango powder)
1 tsp dhania powder
½ tsp garam masala
1 tsp salt or to taste
½ tsp sugar
1 onion - chopped finely
2 green chillies - chopped
some chaat masala to sprinkle

BASTING (POURING ON THE KEBABS)
some melted butter/oil for basting the tikkas

ACHAARI MASALA
1 tbsp saunf (fennel)
½ tsp rai (mustard seeds)
a pinch of methi daana (fenugreek seeds)
½ tsp kalonji (onion seeds), ½ tsp jeera (cumin seeds)

1. Collect seeds of achaari masala- saunf, rai, methi daana, kalonji and jeera together.
2. Heat 2 tbsp oil. Add the collected seeds together to the hot oil. Let saunf change colour.
3. Add onions and chopped green chillies. Cook till onions turn golden brown.
4. Reduce heat. Add haldi, amchoor, dhania powder, garam masala, salt and sugar. Mix. Remove from fire. Let it cool down.
5. Beat curd till smooth. Add garlic-ginger paste and cornflour. Add the onion masala also to the curd.

contd...

6. Add the paneer cubes to the curd. Marinate till serving time.
7. At serving time, rub oil generously over the grill of the oven or wire rack of a gas tandoor. Place paneer on the greased wire rack or grill of the oven.
8. Heat an oven to 180°C or a gas tandoor on moderate flame. Grill paneer for 15 minutes. Spoon some oil or melted butter on the paneer pieces in the oven or tandoor and grill further for 5 minutes.
9. Serve hot sprinkled with chaat masala and dahi poodina chutney (see page 93).

Note:

- The size of tikkas should not be too small. After getting cooked they shrink. A very small piece after getting cooked can turn hard.
- While skewering or placing pieces of vegetables, the pieces should be arranged such that there is atleast 1" gap between them so that each piece can get it's own space and heat all around to get cooked properly.
- Pastes like ginger-garlic paste should be made with minimum water.
- To baste, just pour the oil/melted butter on the food that is being barbecued when it is a little more than half done. It keeps food soft.

Tandoori Makai Mirch

Paneer cubes are mixed with mozzarella cheese to hold the diced paneer and corn together, because on cooking the cheese melts, binding the two together.

Serves 4   *Picture on page 57*

4 medium size capsicums

MARINADE
2 tbsp lemon juice
1 tsp ginger paste
½ tsp garlic paste
1 tbsp oil
¾ tsp salt

STUFFING
100 gm paneer - finely cut into ¼" cubes (1 cup)
½ cup grated mozzarella cheese
½ cup corn kernels - tinned or freshly boiled

contd...

TANDOORI Veg.

1 tbsp chopped cashews and 8-10 kishmish
¼ tsp hing (asafoetida)
1 tsp jeera (cumin seeds) and ½ tsp sarson (mustard seeds)
1 small onion - cut into half and then into rings, to get shredded onion
1 tbsp green coriander - chopped, 2 tbsp oil
½ tsp red chilli powder, ¾ tsp salt
½ tsp garam masala, ¼ tsp amchoor

BASTING
2 tbsp oil or melted butter

1. Cut a slice from the top of each capsicum. Scoop out the center with the help of a knife. Mix all the ingredients of the marinade and rub liberally on the inside of the capsicums. Cover with caps and leave aside for ½ hour.
2. Take a heavy bottom kadhai and heat oil. Put in the hing, jeera, and sarson. Wait till jeera turns golden.
3. Add onions and cook till soft. Add cashews and kishmish. Stir. Add red chilli powder, salt, garam masala and amchoor.

4. Add corn and cook for 1 minute. Add paneer and mix well. Remove from fire. Add coriander and mozzarella cheese. Mix. Keep filling aside.
5. Stuff the capsicums with this filling. They should be stuffed well but not to bursting point. Rub oil on the stuffed capsicums. Cover with the caps and secure them with wooden toothpicks.
6. Oil and wipe the skewers. Skewer the capsicums. Small onions or pieces of potatoes can be used in-between to prevent them from slipping. Put the skewers into the oven or the gas tandoor and cook for 10 minutes or till they turn blackish at some places. Turn 1-2 times in-between to grill evenly. Serve.

Note: Stuffed capsicums can be placed on the wire-rack or grill rubbed with some oil, if you do not have skewers. It is not necessary to fasten them with tooth picks.

Malai Khumb

Picture on facing page   *Serves 6-8*

200 gm mushrooms - choose big ones
juice of ½ lemon
1 tbsp butter - melted, for basting (pouring on the tikkas)
chaat masala to sprinkle

MARINADE
4 tbsp thick cream
1 cup thick curd - hang in a muslin cloth for 15 minutes
2-4 tbsp grated cheese, preferably mozzarella
2 tbsp oil, 1 tbsp cornflour, 1 tbsp ginger paste, ¾ tsp salt
2 tbsp chopped coriander

1. Wash mushrooms well. Trim the stalks neatly.
2. Boil 4-5 cups water with 1 tsp salt and juice of ½ lemon. As soon as the boil comes, add the mushrooms. Let them boil for a minute. Strain and pat dry them on a clean kitchen towel.

contd...

TANDOORI Veg.

3. Squeeze curd and transfer to a bowl. Mix cream, cheese, oil, cornflour, ginger paste, salt and coriander to the hung curd.
4. Marinate the mushrooms in the curd mixture till serving time.
5. To serve, preheat the oven to 180°C. Arrange the marinated mushrooms on a greased wire rack with head side up. Pat the left over marinade on the mushroom heads. You can arrange these on thin skewers also. Grill in a hot oven at 180°C for 10-15 minutes till the coating turns dry.
6. Melt some butter. In between, pour some melted butter on the mushrooms. Grill further for 5-7 minutes or till dry.
7. Remove from oven when done. Sprinkle chaat masala. Serve with dahi poodina chutney (see page 93). Garnish with onion rings.

Note:
- While threading mushrooms, use thin skewers. Push the skewers gently. They should be woven through the vegetable. This way there are less chances of the food slipping down.

Reshmi Paneer Tikka

Extremely soft tikkas cooked in cream.

Serves 4-5

250 gms paneer - cut into 1½" cubes (8 pieces)
3 tbsp besan (gram flour)
2 tbsp curd
1 tsp salt
¼ tsp red chilli powder
½ tsp garam masala
a few drops orange red colour
1 tbsp lemon juice
2 capsicums - cut into 1" pieces
2 onions - cut into 1" pieces
2 tbsp oil

TANDOORI Veg.

GRIND TOGETHER TO A PASTE
½" piece ginger, 3-4 flakes garlic
1 tsp jeera (cumin seeds)
seeds of 2 chhoti illaichi
2-3 green chillies
2 tbsp chopped coriander

FINAL INGREDIENTS
4-5 tbsp thick cream or fresh malai - beaten well till smooth
3-4 tbsp chopped poodina (mint) leaves
1 tsp lemon juice, chaat masala

1. Grind ginger, garlic, jeera, chhoti illaichi, coriander and green chillies to a paste.
2. Add besan, curd, salt, chilli powder, garam masala & lemon juice to the paste. Add enough orange colour to the paste to get a nice colour.
3. Cut paneer into 1½" cubes. Put the paste in a big bowl and add the paneer pieces and mix well so as to coat the paste nicely on all the pieces. Add the onion and capsicum pieces also and mix lightly. Keep aside till serving time.

4. Heat an oven to 180°C or a gas tandoor on moderate flame. Grill the paneer pieces & vegetables by passing through skewers and keeping in a hot oven on a greased wire rack. Keep in the oven for 10-12 minutes. Remove from oven.
5. Heat malai or cream in a clean kadhai on very low flame, to make it just warm. Do not let it turn into ghee by keeping on the fire for a longer time.
6. Add the grilled paneer and vegetable pieces. Toss gently and remove from fire.
7. Serve with garnished papad (see page 102), poodina chutney (see page 94) sprinkled with chopped poodina, chaat masala and lemon juice.

Baby Corn Bullets

Enjoy it rolled up in roomali rotis with some onion slices mixed with hari chutney!

Serves 4-5

200 gm baby corns - keep whole
juice of ½ lemon
1-2 capsicums - cut into 1" pieces
8 cherry tomatoes or 1 large tomato - cut into 8 pieces & pulp removed
1 onion - cut into fours & separated or 4 spring onions (keep white part whole)
1-2 tbsp melted butter for basting
some chaat masala - to sprinkle

MARINADE

1½ cups thick curd - hang for 30 minutes
2 tsp cornflour, 2 tbsp thick cream or malai
¼ tsp ajwain (carom seeds)
1 tbsp thick ginger-garlic paste (squeeze out the liquid)
½ tsp kala namak (black salt), ¼ tsp haldi, 1 tbsp tandoori masala
¼ tsp red chilli powder, ¾ tsp salt

1. Boil 4-5 cups water with 2 tsp salt, ¼ tsp haldi and juice of ½ lemon. Add baby corns to boiling water. After the boil returns, boil for 1 minute or till slightly soft. Strain and wipe dry the corns on a clean kitchen towel. Keep aside.
2. Mix all ingredients of the marinade in a large bowl.
3. Rub oil generously on a wire rack or grill of the oven.
4. Add baby corns first to the marinade in the bowl and mix well to coat the marinade. Remove from bowl and arrange on the greased rack. In the remaining marinade in the bowl, add onion, capsicum & tomatoes. Leave these in the bowl itself. Marinate all for atleast ½ hour.
5. Grill baby corns first in an oven at 200°C for 15 minutes or roast in a gas tandoor. Pour a little melted butter on them. Put the onion and capsicum also along with the corns and grill for another 10 minutes. Lastly put the tomatoes in the oven with the onion-capsicum and grill further for 2-3 minutes.
6. Serve sprinkled with some chat masala, alongwith lemon wedges and chilli garlic chutney (see page 94).

Tandoori Phool

A good meal time side dish.

Serves 4-6

1 medium size gobi (cauliflower) - wash and keep whole with 1-2" stalk

MARINADE
¾ cup thick curd - hang for ½ hour
¼ cup thick cream or malai, 1 tbsp oil
2 tbsp besan - roasted on a tawa for 1 minute or till fragrant
½ tbsp ginger paste
2 tsp tandoori masala
4-6 saboot kali mirch (black peppercorns) - crushed
½ tsp red chilli powder, ¼ tsp haldi, 1 tsp salt

TO SERVE
2 onions - cut into fine rings, 2 tbsp finely chopped coriander
½ tsp chaat masala, 1 tomato - cut into slices

1. Boil 4 cups water with 1 tsp salt.
2. Add cauliflower. When the water starts to boil again, remove from fire. Let the cauliflower be in hot water for 3-4 minutes. Remove from water and keep aside.
3. Wipe the cauliflower with a clean kitchen towel. Keep aside.
4. Mix together in a bowl all ingredients of the marinade. Insert the marinade inside the cauliflower florets, from the bottom also. Rub the top of the flower with the left over marinade. Keep aside for at least 1 hour.
5. Brush the grilling rack of the oven generously with oil. Place the marinated cauliflower on the greased grilling rack.
6. Grill in a hot oven at 200°C for 30 minutes or more till brown specs appear on the cauliflower. Keep aside till serving time.
7. To serve, cut the whole cauliflower into 4 big pieces right through the stalk. Cut each piece further into 2 pieces. Sprinkle chaat masala.
8. Add fresh coriander and chaat masala to the onions.
9. To serve, heat gobi in an oven or microwave till really hot. Arrange the pieces neatly in a serving platter. Sprinkle lime juice. Garnish with onion rings & tomato slices. Serve with poodina chutney (page 94).

TANDOORI Veg.

Haryali Paneer Tikka

Paneer tikka coated with a green coloured chutney.

Picture on facing page   Serves 6

400 gm paneer - cut into 1½" long pieces, 1" thick
4 tbsp besan (gram flour), 1 tsp salt
4 tbsp oil

GRIND TO A FINE PASTE (CHUTNEY)
1 cup fresh green dhania (green coriander)
1 green chilli, 2 tsp saunf (fennel), 5-6 flakes garlic, 1" piece ginger
4 tbsp lemon juice
½ tsp salt

1. Grind together dhania, green chilli, saunf, ginger, garlic, lemon juice
and salt to a fine paste.

contd...

Roomali Rooti : Recipe on page 90 ➤
Dal Makhani : Recipe on page 98, Haryali Paneer Tikka ➤

TANDOORI Veg.

2. Slit the paneer pieces and keep aside.
3. Divide the chutney into 2 parts.
4. With one part of the chutney, stuff some chutney in the slits of all the paneer pieces. Keep the stuffed paneer aside.
5. Mix together the left over chutney, besan, salt and 4 tbsp oil. Rub this all over the stuffed paneer pieces.
6. Rub some oil generously over the grill of the oven or wire rack of a gas tandoor. Place paneer on the greased wire rack or grill of the oven.
7. Heat an oven to 180°C or a gas tandoor on moderate flame. Grill paneer for 15 minutes. Spoon some drops of oil or melted butter on the paneer pieces in the oven or tandoor and grill further for 5 minutes. Serve hot with peanut cabbage relish (see page 96) & poodina chutney.

Note:
- To cook the tikkas in the oven, place a drip tray under the wire rack on which the tikkas are placed, to collect the drippings.
- While skewering or placing the tikka the pieces should be arranged such that there is atleast 1" gap between them so that each piece can get it's own space and heat all around to get cooked properly.

Tandoori Bharwaan Aloo

Serves 6   *Picture on page 2*

3 big (longish) potatoes
some chaat masala to sprinkle

FILLING

3 almonds - crushed with a belan (rolling pin)
4 tbsp grated paneer (50 gm)
1 tbsp poodina (mint) leaves - chopped
1 green chilli - deseeded and chopped
¼ tsp garam masala
¼ tsp red chilli powder
¼ tsp salt or to taste
a pinch amchoor

COVERING

½ cup thick curd - hang in a muslin cloth for 30 minutes

TANDOORI Veg.

1 tbsp ginger paste
¼ tsp red chilli powder
¾ tsp salt
¼ tsp red or orange tandoori colour or haldi

CRUSH TOGETHER TO A ROUGH POWDER
1 tsp shah jeera (black cumin)
seeds of 2 moti illaichi (brown cardamom)
2-3 blades of javetri (mace)
6-8 saboot kali mirch (peppercorns)

1. Boil potatoes in salted water till just tender. Do not over boil. When they are no longer hot, peel skin.
2. Mix crushed almonds with mint leaves, green chillies, 4 tbsp grated paneer, ¼ tsp salt, ¼ tsp garam masala, ¼ tsp red chilli and a pinch of amchoor.
3. Grind or crush shah jeera, seeds of moti illaichi, peppercorns and 2-3 pinches of javetri to a coarse powder.
4. To the paneer mixture, add ¼-½ teaspoon of the above freshly ground spice powder also. Keep the leftover powder aside.

5. Mix hung curd, ginger paste, the left over freshly ground powder and red chilli powder and salt. Add haldi or orange colour.
6. Run the tip of a fork on the surface of the potatoes, making the surface rough. (The rough surface holds the masalas well).
7. Cut each potato into 2 halves, vertically. Scoop out, just a little, to get a small cavity in each potato with the back of a teaspoon. Stuff with paneer filling.
8. With a spoon apply the curd mixture on the outside (backside) of the potatoes and on the rim also (not on the filling).
9. Grill potatoes in a gas tandoor or a preheated oven at 180°C/400°F for 15 minutes on a greased wire rack till they get slightly dry.
10. Spoon some oil or melted butter on them (baste) and then grill further for 10 minutes till the coating turns absolutely dry.
11. Sprinkle some chaat masala and serve hot with dahi poodina chutney (see page 93) and garnished papad (see page 102).

Note: Must baste the tikkas, atleast once in between grilling. To baste, just pour the oil/melted butter on the food that is being barbecued when it is a little more than half done. It keeps food soft.

Arbi Tandoori

Try this different way of preparing arbi for dinner tonight!

Serves 4

½ kg arbi (calocassia) - medium size

MARINADE

1 cup curd - hang in a muslin cloth for ½ hour
1 tbsp tandoori masala
1 tsp ginger paste, 6-8 peppercorns - crushed
½ tsp ajwain, a pinch of haldi
1 tbsp oil
½ tsp salt, 1 tbsp besan

OTHER INGREDIENTS

3 tbsp oil, 1 tsp crushed saboot dhania (coriander seeds)
4-5 onions - cut into rings, ½ tsp garam masala, ¼ tsp salt, or to taste
1½ tsp amchoor (dried mango powder), 3-4 green chillies - slit lengthwise
½" piece ginger - shredded

1. Hang curd in a muslin cloth for ½ hour.
2. Boil arbi in salted water with ½ tsp of amchoor, till soft. Peel and flatten the pieces.
3. Mix tandoori masala, ginger paste and crushed saboot kali mirch to hung curd. Add ajwain, a pinch of haldi for colour and 1 tbsp oil. Add ½ tsp salt and besan.
4. Heat an oven to 180°C or a gas tandoor on moderate flame. Grease the wire rack well. Dip arbi pieces in the prepared curd and arrange on the greased rack.
5. Grill for 15 minutes. When coating turns a little dry, baste (pour) with some oil. Grill further for 15 minutes or till the curd dries up and forms a coating and arbi turns brownish. Keep arbi aside.
6. Heat 3 tbsp oil. Add crushed saboot dhania. Wait till it turns golden. Add onion rings. Cook till onions turn light brown.
7. Add garam masala, amchoor and salt. Add the arbi.
8. Add shredded ginger & green chillies. Mix well. Stir fry for 3-4 minutes.
9. Remove from fire. Serve hot with poodina chutney (see page 94) and garnished papad (see page 102).

Tamatar Baingan Wale

Stuffed tomatoes are irresistible, both to the eye and to the palate.
They make excellent starters to any meal.

Serves 6

6 large firm red tomatoes, 1 tsp ginger - garlic paste

STUFFING

1 large round brinjal (bharte waala baingan) - roasted on a gas flame
1 tsp jeera (cumin seeds), 3 tbsp oil, ¾ tsp salt
2 tomatoes - chopped, 2 tbsp chopped coriander leaves

GROUND TO A PASTE

2 onions, 2 tbsp roughly chopped coriander, 6 green chillies

BATTER

½ cup besan (gram flour)
½ cup thick cream, ½ -1 cup milk
1 tsp dhania powder (coriander powder), ½ tsp salt

1. Rub a little oil over the baingan and roast over a gas flame until the skin gets charred and starts to peel off and the flesh is soft.
2. Remove the charred skin of baingan. Wash and chop roughly.
3. Heat oil in kadhai, add jeera let it change colour. Add the ground onion paste. Cook for 3-4 minutes or till golden brown.
4. Add the roughly chopped baingan. Bhuno for 4-5 minutes or till tender.
5. Add the chopped tomatoes and salt. Cook till the mixture leaves oil.
6. Wash and pat dry the whole tomatoes. Slice the top (cap) and scoop out the pulp carefully. Rub the ginger- garlic paste well on the inside of the tomatoes. Fill in the brinjal mixture, close the top (cap) with the help of a toothpick.
7. Mix all the ingredients of the batter. Dip the tomatoes in this batter. Coat well.
8. Grill tomatoes in a preheated oven at 180°C for 10 minutes on a greased wire rack till they get slightly dry.
9. When coating turns dry, spoon some oil on them (baste) and then grill further for 5 minutes till the coating turns absolutely dry.
10. Sprinkle some chaat masala and serve hot with dahi poodina chutney (see page 93) and garnished papad (see page 102).

Tandoori Gobhi

Picture on facing page   *Serves* 12

500 gm (2 medium heads) cauliflower - cut into medium sized florets with
small stalks
chaat masala and lemon wedges

MARINADE

1 cup thick curd - hang for 15 minutes or more and squeeze to remove all water
1 tbsp kasoori methi (dry fenugreek leaves)
1 tbsp besan (gram flour) - dry roasted on a tawa (griddle) on low heat till
fragrant, for about 1 minute
1 tbsp oil
1 tbsp ginger-garlic paste
½ tsp red chilli powder
¼ tsp haldi
1 tsp salt
¼ tsp kala namak (black salt)
1 tsp tandoori masala

TANDOORI Veg.

1. Boil 5-6 cups of water in a large pan. Add 2 tsp salt and 1 tsp sugar to the water. Add gobhi pieces to the boiling water. After the boil returns, remove from fire. Leave in hot water for 10-15 minutes. Drain. Refresh with cold water. Strain. Wipe the pieces well with a clean kitchen towel till well dried.
2. Mix all the ingredients of the marinade in a large pan. Add the gobhi to it and mix well. Keep in the refrigerator till the time of serving.
3. To serve, rub the grill of the oven with some oil. Place the gobhi on it. Grill for 10-15 minutes. Do not over grill it, it turns too dry.
4. Serve hot with poodina chutney (see page 94) and garnished papad (See page 102). Serve hot sprinkled with chaat masala and lemon wedges.

Tandoori Kathal

Serves 6   *Picture on page 1*

300 gms of kathal (jack fruit), a pinch of haldi

MARINADE
1 cup thick curd - hang in a muslin cloth for 30 minutes
1 tbsp tandoori masala
1 tbsp ginger paste
¼ tsp red chilli powder
1 tbsp oil
¾ tsp salt
a pinch of tandoori colour or haldi

CRUSH TOGETHER TO A ROUGH POWDER
½ tsp bhuna jeera (roasted cumin)
seeds of 2 chhoti illaichi (brown cardamom)
2-3 blades of javetri (mace)
3-4 saboot kali mirch (peppercorns)

41

TANDOORI Veg.

1. Rub oil on your hands. Cut the whole big piece of kathal from the middle into two pieces. Remove skin. Cut widthwise from the centre of each piece. This way you get two big strips of kathal. Now further divide each strip into smaller pieces about 1" thickness, carefully to keep the shreds of the piece together. Then further divide into ½" thick pieces.
2. Boil 7- 8 cups of water with 2 tsp salt and a pinch of haldi. Add kathal and boil for 10 minutes till crisp-tender. Keep aside.
3. Grind or crush shah jeera, seeds of chhoti illaichi, peppercorns and 2-3 pinches of javetri to a coarse powder.
4. Mix all the ingredients of the marinade, freshly ground spice powder and kathal. Let it marinate for an hour in the refrigerator.
5. Grill kathal in a gas tandoor or a preheated oven at 180°C for 15 minutes on a greased wire rack till the coating gets slightly dry.
6. Spoon some oil or melted butter on it (baste) & grill further for 10 minutes till coating turns absolutely dry. Sprinkle some chaat masala.
7. Serve hot with poodina chutney (see page 94) and garnished papad (see page 102).

Moong Stuffed Tinda

Serves 4

500 gm (8-10) tinda - firm, medium sized
½ tsp salt, juice of 1 lemon, 2 tsp ginger paste
2 tsp dhania powder, ½ tsp garam masala, ¼ tsp red chilli powder, ½ tsp haldi

FILLING

75 gm (½ cup) dhuli moong dal - soaked for 2 hours & drained in a strainer
½ cup (50 gm) grated paneer, 1 tbsp desi ghee or oil
a pinch of hing (asafoetida), ½ tsp jeera (cumin seeds)
1 green chilli - finely chopped, ½" piece ginger - finely chopped
½ tsp dhania powder, ½ tsp red chilli powder, ¼ tsp haldi, ¾ tsp salt

1. Wash & scrape tindas. Cut a thin slice from top. Keep the slice (cap) aside. Scoop out tindas to make them hollow. Do not scoop to much.
2. Mix salt, lime juice & ginger. Rub this on the inside & outside of tindas.
3. For filling - heat 1 tbsp ghee or oil in a heavy bottomed kadhai. Add a pinch of hing. Wait for 5-10 seconds. Add jeera. Let it change colour.
4. Reduce flame. Add ginger and green chilli. Mix.

contd...

5. Add dhania powder, red chilli powder and haldi.
6. Add dal. Add salt to taste and cook covered on low flame for about 5-7 minutes. Do not overcook the dal, as it has to be grilled further. Sprinkle a little water in-between, if it sticks to the bottom of the kadhai.
7. Add paneer and mix well. Remove from fire. Keep filling aside.
8. Heat 3 tbsp oil in a kadhai. Add ½ tsp jeera and fry till golden.
9. Reduce flame and add 2 tsp dhania powder, ½ tsp garam masala, ¼ tsp red chilli powder and ½ tsp haldi.
10. Add scopped tindas (without filling) & their caps one by one. Gently turn them, to coat oil all over. Cook for 2 minutes turning sides gently.
11. Stuff the dal filling inside the fried tindas. Press well. Cover with the fired cap. Secure the cap with a toothpick.
12. Heat an oven to 200°C or a gas tandoor on moderate flame.
13. Rub oil generously over grill or wire rack of the oven or gas tandoor. Place the stuffed tindas on the greased wire rack or grill of the oven, leaving the masala oil behind in the kadhai.
14. Grill tindas for 5 minutes, till they feel soft when a knife is inserted in them. Spoon some masala oil or melted butter on the tindas in the oven or gas tandoor and grill further for 5 minutes. Serve hot.

Tandoori Bharwaan Lauki

Serves 4-5

500 gm lauki (bottle gourd) - medium thickness

FILLING
200 gm paneer - crumbled (mash roughly)
1 tsp finely chopped ginger, 1 green chilli - finely chopped
2 tbsp chopped green coriander
8-10 kaju (cashewnuts) - chopped
8-10 kishmish (raisins) - soaked in water
¾ tsp salt or to taste

MARINADE
1 cup thick curd - hang for 30 minutes in a muslin cloth
¼ cup thick cream or malai, 1 tbsp oil
2 tbsp besan - roasted on a tawa for 1 minute or till fragrant
½ tbsp ginger paste, 2 tsp tandoori masala
4-6 saboot kali mirch (black peppercorns) - crushed
½ tsp red chilli powder, ¼ tsp haldi, 1 tsp salt

TANDOORI Veg.

1. Peel lauki. Cut vertically into 2 pieces from centre to get 2 smaller pieces.
2. Boil in salted water, covered, for about 5 minutes. Do not over boil the lauki. Remove from water and cool.
3. Scoop seeds from both the pieces of the lauki and make them hollow.
4. Mix all the ingredients of the filling. Mix well.
5. Stuff it into the boiled lauki pieces. Keep aside.
6. Mix all the ingredients of the marinade .
7. With a spoon apply the marinade on the outside of the lauki and on the sides. Do not apply on the filling (top). Keep aside for an hour.
8. Grill lauki in a gas tandoor or a preheated oven at 180°C/350°F for 5 minutes on a greased wire rack. Grill till the coating get slightly dry.
9. Spoon some oil or melted butter on it (baste) and then change side. Grill further for 5 minutes till the coating turns absolutely dry.
10. Cut the prepared lauki into ¾" thick round pieces. Transfer to a serving dish, sprinkle some chaat and serve with chilli garlic chutney (pg 94).

Bhein Tandoori

The water vegetable - lotus stem is coated with a white yogurt paste and grilled.

Serves 4

300 gm (2 medium) bhein or kamal kakri (lotus stem) - cut into diagonal
thick pieces
3 onions - each cut into 4 pieces and separated
1 tsp ajwain (carom seeds)
¼ tsp haldi, ¼ tsp salt, ¼ tsp red chilli powder
2-3 tbsp chopped coriander, 2 tbsp oil

MARINADE
1½ cups curd - hang for ½ hour
1 tsp ajwain (carom seeds)
1 tbsp finely chopped coriander
1½ tbsp besan (gram flour)
1 tbsp ginger garlic paste
1 tbsp oil
1 tsp salt

TANDOORI Veg.

½ tsp red chilli powder
½ tsp haldi
1½ tsp dhania powder
½ tsp garam masala

1. Peel bhein. Cut into diagonal pieces of 1½" thickness.
2. Put bhein in a pan with 3-4 cups water and 1 tsp salt. Keep on fire. Boil. Reduce heat and cook covered for about 10 minutes on low heat. Remove from fire. Strain and pat dry.
3. Mix all ingredients of the marinade. Mix well.
4. Add the boiled pieces of bhein and onions to the marinade. Mix well to coat nicely. Keep aside for an hour.
5. Grill bhein and onions in a preheated oven at 180°C for 10-15 minutes on a greased wire rack or grill till the coating turns slightly dry.
6. Spoon some oil or melted butter on it (baste) and then grill further for 5 minutes till the coating turns absolutely dry.
7. Serve hot with poodina chutney (see page 94), sprinkled with chaat masala and chopped coriander.

Baingan Tikka

Serves 6   *Picture on inside front cover*

750 gms (7-8) brinjals of long thin variety and sprinkled with salt
20 small onions or 5 onions - cut into four

MARINADE
1 cup yogurt - hang in a muslin cloth for ½ hour
1 tbsp vinegar
2 tbsp ginger-garlic paste
½ onion - ground to a paste
1 tbsp kasoori methi (dry fenugreek leaves)
1 tsp jeera - powdered (cumin powder)
2 tsp red chilli powder
2 tbsp oil
2 tsp salt
1 tsp red tandoori colour or haldi

BASTING
2 tbsp melted butter or oil

GARNISH
onion rings, lemon

1. Wash baingans and cut each brinjal into half lengthwise and then into 2" pieces. Sprinkle with salt and keep aside for 15 minutes.
2. Pat dry the brinjals sprinkled with salt on a clean kitchen towel.
3. Mix all the ingredients of the marinade. Add the brinjal tikkas and onions. Let them marinate for an hour.
4. Heat an oven to 180°C. Place the baingan pieces on a greased wire grill OR oil and wipe the skewers. Skewer the marinated baingan tikkas with small onions in between. Grill for 15 minutes.
5. Baste (pour) the tikkas with melted butter or oil and grill further for 15 minutes or till coating turns absolutely dry. Check with a knife, the tikkas should be tender, if not, then grill further for 5 minutes.
6. Serve hot with poodina chutney (see page 94). Garnish with lemon wedges.

SEEKHS

Bhutte Ke Seekh

Corn is very popular in India. Here corn makes a crunchy kebab.

Makes 7-8 pieces

4 tender, large fresh bhuttas - grated (1 cup) or 1 cup tinned or frozen corn -
blend ½ of the tinned or frozen corn in a mixer and keep ½ whole kernels
2 potatoes - boiled & grated
1 onion - chopped
2 green chillies - chopped finely
2 tbsp chopped fresh coriander
½ tbsp chopped mint (poodina)
½ tsp garam masala powder
1 tbsp melted butter
½ tsp pepper powder
1 tsp salt or to taste
3 tbsp besan (gramflour) - roasted on a tawa for 1 minute till fragrant
juice of 1 lemon
3 tbsp melted butter for basting (pouring on the kebabs)

1. Mash the boiled potatoes and the corn. Mix well.
2. Add onions, green chillies, coriander, mint, garam masala, 1 tbsp melted butter, salt and pepper. Check seasoning.
3. Add roasted besan and lemon juice.
4. Oil and wipe the skewers. Heat an oven to 180°C or a gas tandoor on moderate flame for 15 minutes.
5. Press mixture into sausage-shaped kebabs on the skewers, making a long kebab of the corn paste over the skewer. Cook for about 5 minutes in a hot tandoor or grill. Pour some melted butter on the kebabs to baste them when they get half done. Turn side and grill for 8-10 minutes or till golden brown.
6. Serve with chilli garlic chutney (see page 94) and peanut cabbage relish (see page 96).

Note: If you wish you could even shallow fry the kebabs in a pan on medium heat in 3 tbsp oil.

Gulnar Seekh Kebab

Picture on page 2   *Makes 15*

1 cup saboot masoor ki dal
1" piece ginger
8-10 flakes garlic
1 green chilli - chopped
1 tsp jeera, 1 tsp garam masala
1 tsp red chilli powder, ¼ tsp amchoor
½ cup mashed paneer
3 tbsp cornflour
½ piece of a bread churned in a mixer to get fresh bread crumbs
1 tsp salt or to taste
1-2 tsp lemon juice
3 tbsp oil
4 tbsp of each capsicum, onion and tomato (without pulp) - finely chopped

TO SERVE
2 onions - cut into rings, juice of 1 lemon, poodina chutney

1. Soak saboot masoor dal for 2 hours. Strain.
2. Grind dal, ginger, garlic, green chilli and jeera to a thick smooth paste using the minimum amount of water. Keep dal paste aside.
3. Heat 3 tbsp oil in a heavy bottomed kadhai. Add dal. Stir-fry for 4-5 minutes on low flame till dal is dry and does not stick to the bottom of the kadhai. Remove from fire.
4. Mix cornflour, paneer, salt, garam masala, bread crumbs, red chilli powder and amchoor with the dal. Add lemon juice and 2 tbsp of the chopped vegetables. Reserve the remaining half. Mix well. Keep aside.
5. Heat 3-4 tbsp oil on a tawa or a nonstick pan for shallow frying.
6. Grease a skewer. Spread a ball of dal paste to make a 2" long kebab of the dal paste over the skewer or a pencil.
7. Stick the remaining 2 tbsp of finely chopped onion, capsicum and tomatoes (without pulp) on the kebab by pressing onions etc. with the palm on to the kebab. Gently pull out the skewer or a pencil and shallow fry the seekh in medium hot oil to a light brown colour.
8. Serve with dahi poodina chutney (see page 93) and garnished papad (see page 102) on a bed of onion rings sprinkled with lemon juice.

Subz Kakori

Very soft and delicious vegetarian seekh kebabs.

Picture on facing page   *Serves 4-5*

3 potatoes (medium) - boiled
(250 gm) 2 cups jimikand (yam) - chopped and boiled
½ cup crumbled paneer
4 tbsp kaju (cashewnuts) - ground
1 tsp ginger paste, 1 tsp garlic paste, 1 big onion - very finely chopped (1 cup)
2 green chillies - very finely chopped
2 tbsp green coriander - very finely chopped
1 tsp bhuna jeera (cumin roasted), 1 tsp red chilli powder, ¼ tsp amchoor
2 bread slices - crumbled in a grinder to get fresh crumbs
1½ tsp salt, or to taste, a pinch of tandoori red colour
Basting - 2 tbsp melted butter or oil
Garnish - Tandoori khatta masala or chaat masala

Tandoori Makai Mirch : Recipe on page 15, Subz Kakori ➢

TANDOORI Veg.

1. Boil the potatoes. Peel and mash.
2. Pressure cook chopped yam with ½ cup water and ½ tsp salt to give 3 whistles. Remove from fire. After the pressure drops, keep it on fire to dry, if there is any excess water. Mash it to a paste.
3. Mix mashed potatoes, yam and all other ingredients, making a slightly stiff dough.
4. Oil and wipe the skewers. Heat the gas tandoor or oven. Remove the wire rack. Press into sausage-shaped kebabs on the skewers and cook for about 5 minutes in a hot oven at 180°C or a gas tandoor. Pour some melted butter on the kebabs to baste them when they get half done. Turn side and grill for 5-7 minutes or till golden brown. If you do not wish to grill the kebabs, shallow fry in 2 tbsp oil in a pan on low heat, turning sides till browned evenly.
5. Sprinkle some tandoori or chaat masala and serve with onion rings and lemon wedges. Serve hot with poodina chutney (see page 94).

Note: Turn kebabs on the skewers only after they are half done, otherwise they tend to break.

Hari Seekh Salaad

An unusual, roasted green salad on skewers. Good to start the meal!

Serves 6   *Picture on page 75*

12 big spinach leaves
1 medium broccoli - broken into small florets
5 whole, white part of spring onions, choose big ones
12 cabbage leaves - separated

MARINADE

1¼ cups yogurt - hang for ½ hour in a muslin cloth
1 onion - grind to a paste
1 tbsp freshly ground pepper
1 tsp garam masala
½ tsp amchoor
1½ tbsp oil, 1¼ tsp salt

BASTING

left over marinade

TANDOORI Veg.

1. Clean and wash all the vegetables. Pat dry the spinach and cabbage leaves on a clean kitchen towel.
2. Boil 4 cups water with 1 tsp salt and 1 tsp sugar. Add broccoli. Let it come to a boil. Boil for 1 minute. Remove from fire. Let it be in hot water for 5 minutes. Drain and refresh in cold water. Wipe dry on a clean kitchen towel.
3. Mix all the ingredients of the marinade – yogurt, onion paste, pepper, garam masala, amchoor, and 1½ tbsp oil.
4. Take one vegetable at a time and spread the marinade on each vegetable or leaf on both the sides thoroughly. Mix well, leave aside for 1 hour mixing atleast twice in between.
5. Oil and wipe the skewers. Heat the oven at 180°C or gas tandoor on moderate heat.
6. Skewer the vegetables - thread them starting with broccoli, then fold a cabbage leaf and insert, fold a spinach leaf once and then fold again (like a pan) and insert, then insert a whole spring onion and then again another folded cabbage leaf and spinach leaf in the same skewer,

repeating till the skewer gets fully covered (cabbage and spinach leaf have been threaded twice).

7. Spread the left over marinade on the skewered vegetables with hand.
8. Put the skewers in the oven or tandoor and cook for 2 minutes.
9. Take out the skewer carefully and baste them again with the marinade. Put them back into the tandoor or oven. Cook for 5 minutes.
10. Serve hot with chilli garlic chutney (see page 94) and peanut cabbage relish (see page 96).

KEBABS

Poodina Kaju Kebabs

Cashew kebabs stuffed with a minty filling.

Serves 6-8

15 kaju (cashewnuts) - ground to a coarse powder in a small spice grinder
4 slices of bread - broken into pieces and ground in a mixer to get fresh
crumbs
2 big potatoes - chopped
2 small onions - chopped
¾ cup shelled peas
½ of a small cauliflower - cut into small florets
1" piece ginger - crushed to a paste
5-6 flakes garlic - crushed to a paste
½ tsp red chilli powder, ½ tsp garam masala, 1½ tsp salt or to taste
2 tsp tomato sauce
1 green chilli - finely chopped
2 tbsp chopped fresh coriander
4 tbsp cornflour

TANDOORI Veg.

FILLING
2-3 tbsp very finely chopped poodina, ½ small onion - chopped finely
¼ tsp amchoor, ¼ tsp salt

1. Pressure cook potatoes, cauliflower, onion and peas with 1 cup water to give 2 whistles. Keep on low flame for 5 minutes. Remove from fire. Cool. Drain and leave in a sieve for about 5 minutes to remove excess moisture.
2. Mash the vegetables and add ginger, garlic, red chilli powder, garam masala, salt and tomato sauce.
3. Add green chilli, fresh coriander, cornflour, cashewnuts and fresh bread crumbs.
4. Mix all ingredients of the filling together. Keep aside.
5. Break off small balls of the vegetable mixture and pat them into flat circular shapes about ½" thick, with wet hands.
6. Stuff a little of the filling and form a ball. Shape again into a flat disc.
7. Heat 4-5 tbsp oil in a frying pan or on a tawa and fry gently over medium heat, turning once.
8. Remove on paper napkin to remove excess oil. Serve hot.

Dal Poodina Kebab

Delicious and quick to prepare.

Serves 10-12

1½ cups channe ki dal
1 tsp salt
½" piece ginger, 4-5 flakes garlic
2½ cups water
4 slices bread - broken into pieces and churned in a mixer to get fresh crumbs
½ tsp garam masala
½ tsp amchoor (dried mango powder)
2-3 tbsp maida (plain flour) - to coat

FILLING
2-3 tbsp very finely chopped poodina
1 small onion - chopped finely
1 green chilli - chopped finely
¼ tsp amchoor
¼ tsp salt

TANDOORI Veg.

1. Clean, wash dal. Pressure cook dal, salt, ginger, garlic and 2½ cups water together. After the first whistle, keep the cooker on low flame for 15 minutes.
2. After the pressure drops down, mash the dal while it is hot, with a karchhi. Keep aside.
3. Add fresh bread crumbs, amchoor and garam masala to the boiled and mashed dal. Add salt to taste. Keep aside.
4. Mix all ingredients of the filling in a small bowl.
5. Make marble sized balls of the dal paste. Flatten them. Put ½ tsp of poodina mixture. Form a ball again. Flatten to form a kebab.
6. Roll in maida and deep fry 3-4 pieces at a time.
7. Dot each kebab with dahi poodina chutney with a spoon (see page 93). Serve with garnished papad (see page 102). Sprinkle chaat masala.

Note: If the kebabs break on frying, add 1-2 tbsp of maida to the mixture.

Kebab Hara Bhara

Serves 8

1 cup channe ki dal (split gram)
1 bundle (600 gm) spinach - only leaves, chopped very finely
3 tbsp oil
3 slices bread - broken into pieces and churned in a mixer to get fresh crumbs
3 tbsp cornflour, 2 green chillies - chopped finely
½ tsp red chilli powder, ½ tsp garam masala, ¾ tsp salt or to taste
½ tsp amchoor (dried mango powder)
½ cup grated paneer (75 gm), ¼ cup chopped green coriander

CRUSH TOGETHER

½ tsp jeera, seeds of 2 moti illaichi, 3-4 saboot kali mirch, 2-3 laung

1. Crush jeera, seeds of moti illaichi, kali mirch and laung together.
2. Clean, wash dal. Pressure cook dal with the above crushed spices, ½ tsp salt and 2 cups water. After the first whistle, keep the cooker on slow fire for 15 minutes. Remove from fire and keep aside.

contd...

3. After the pressure drops down, mash the hot dal with a karchhi or a potato masher. If there is any water, mash the dal on fire and dry the dal as well while you are mashing it. Remove from fire.

4. Discard stem of spinach and chop leaves very finely. Wash in several changes of water. Leave the chopped spinach in the strainer for 15 minutes so that the water drains out.

5. Heat 3 tbsp oil in a kadhai. Squeeze and add spinach. Stir for 8-10 minutes till spinach is absolutely dry and well fried.

6. Add paneer and coriander. Cook for 1 minute. Remove from fire and keep aside.

7. Mix dal with - fresh bread crumbs, cornflour, spinach-paneer, green chillies, salt and masalas. Make small balls. Flatten slightly.

8. Cook them on a tawa with just 2-3 tbsp oil till brown on both sides. When done shift them on the sides of the tawa so that they turn crisp and the oil drains out while more kebabs can be added to the hot oil in the centre of the tawa. Remove the kebabs on paper napkins.

9. Serve hot with dahi poodina chutney (see page 93).

Note: If the kebabs break on frying, roll them in dry maida before frying.

Hare Chholia Ke Kebab

There are unlimited combinations for making vegetable kebabs, here fresh green gram has been used to churn out deliciously succulent kebabs.

Makes 14   *Picture on page 103*

2 cups fresh green gram (hara chholia)
½ cup besan (gramflour) - roasted on a tawa for 2-3 minutes, or till fragrant
2 slices bread - broken into pieces and churned in a mixer to get fresh crumbs
1 cup yogurt - hang in a muslin cloth for 30 minutes
1 small onion - chopped, 1 tbsp ginger-garlic paste
3-4 green chillies - chopped, 10-12 fresh curry leaves
1 tbsp tandoori masala, 1 tsp salt or to taste
1 tsp jeera
3 tbsp oil plus oil for shallow frying
2-3 tbsp maida (plain flour)

CRUSH TOGETHER
1 tbsp saboot dhania (coriander seeds), 1 tsp roasted jeera (bhuna jeera)
½ tsp saboot kali mirch (black peppercorns)

TANDOORI Veg.

1. Crush saboot dhania, bhuna jeera and saboot kali mirch on a chakla-belan (rolling board-pin).
2. Clean, wash hara chholia. Pressure cook hara chhole with the above crushed spices, ½ tsp salt and 1 cup water. Give one whistle. Remove from fire and keep aside. After the pressure drops down, mash the hot hara chholia with a potato masher or a karchhi. If there is any water, mash and dry the chholia on fire. Remove from fire.
3. Heat 3 tbsp oil, add jeera, let it change colour. Add chopped onion, ginger-garlic paste, chopped green chillies and curry leaves. Cook till onions turn light brown.
4. Add mashed chholia, salt, roasted besan, tandoori masala and hung yogurt. Cook for 5 minutes or till dry. Remove from fire. Cool.
5. Add bread crumbs and mix well.
6. Make marble sized balls of the chholia mixture. Flatten to form a kebab of about 2" diameter.
7. Roll in maida and shallow fry 3-4 pieces at a time on a hot tawa in 6 tbsp oil. Turn sides till both sides are crisp. Remove the kebabs on paper napkins. Serve.

Special Shami Kebab

Serves 4

½ cup kale channe (black gram)
1 tbsp channe ki dal (bengal gram split)
1 onion - very finely chopped
1 tsp oil
1 tsp ginger paste, ½ tsp garlic paste
2 slices bread - grind in a mixer to get fresh crumbs
salt to taste
¼ tsp amchoor (dried mango powder)

GRIND TOGETHER TO A COARSE POWDER

¼ tsp jeera, 1" stick dalchini
3-4 laung (cloves)
3-4 saboot kali mirch (peppercorns), seeds of 2 moti illaichi
1 dry, red chilli

FILLING

2 tbsp finely chopped mint (poodina), 4 tbsp grated mozzarella cheese

TANDOORI Veg.

1. Soak kale channe with channe ki dal overnight or for 6-8 hours in water.
2. Put kale channe, channe ki dal, onion and oil in a pressure cooker. Add powdered spices and 1½ cups water also. Pressure cook to give 1 whistle. After the first whistle, keep on slow fire for 20 minutes. Remove from fire and let the pressure drop by itself.
3. If there is extra water, dry the channas for sometime on fire. There should just be a little water, enough to grind the channas to a fine paste.
4. Grind to a fine paste.
5. Remove channa mixture to a bowl. Add ginger-garlic paste, bread, salt and amchoor to taste.
6. Mix all ingredients of the filling together.
7. Make a small ball of the paste. Flatten it, put 1 tsp of filling. Press the filling. Pick up the sides and make a ball again. Flatten it slightly.
8. Shallow fry 4-5 pieces on a tawa in 3-4 tbsp oil on medium flame.
9. Serve with poodina chutney and garnished papad (see page 102).

Note: If the kebabs break on frying, roll in dry maida alone or in egg white first and then in maida. Fry on moderate heat.

Matar Makhane ke Kebab

Delicious crunchy green kebabs. Very appetizing to look at!

Makes 8 kebabs

1 cup boiled or frozen shelled peas (matar)
1 cup makhanas (puffed lotus seeds)
1 tbsp oil
2 green chillies - chopped
2-3 tbsp cashewnuts (kaju)
¾ tsp salt or to taste, ½ tsp pepper
¼ tsp garam masala, seeds of 4-5 chhoti illaichi (green cardamoms)

1. Heat 1 tbsp oil in kadhai. Add makhanas and saute for 3-4 minutes.
2. Add cashewnuts and saute till cashews start changing colour. Remove makhanas and cashewnuts from the kadhai.
3. In the same kadhai (without any oil leftover), add peas and saute for 2 minutes. Remove peas from kadhai.

contd...

TANDOORI Veg.

4. Grind makhanas and kaju together to a rough powder.
5. Grind peas with green chillies to a fine paste.
6. Mix makhanas and pea paste. Add salt, pepper, garam masala and chhoti illaichi.
7. Makes small balls and flatten them to get small round kebabs (tikkis).
8. Shallow fry on tawa or pan in 1-2 tbsp oil till brown and crisp.
9. Sprinkle chaat masala and serve hot with chilli garlic chutney (see page 94) and peanut cabbage relish (see page 96).

Hari Seekh Salaad : Recipe on page 59 ➢

Other Tandoori Delicacies

Exotic Veg Platter and Barbecue Sauce

Serves 8

250 gm paneer - cut into large (1½") cubes
200 gm (10) large mushrooms - trim ends of the stalks, leaving them whole
100 gm babycorns - blanched with a pinch of haldi and 1 tsp salt in 3 cups water
2 capsicums - cut into large cubes
8 cherry tomatoes or 1 large tomato - cut into 8 pieces & pulp removed
1 large onion - cut into fours & separated

MARINADE

1 cup thick curd - hang for 30 minutes in a muslin cloth
2 tbsp thick cream, 2 tbsp oil, 1 tbsp cornflour
1 tbsp thick ginger-garlic paste, ½ tsp black salt
¼ tsp haldi or tandoori colour, 2 tsp tandoori masala
½ tsp red chilli powder, ¾ tsp salt or to taste

BARBECUE SAUCE

3 tbsp butter or oil, 4-5 flakes garlic - crushed
2 large tomatoes - pureed till smooth, ¼ cup ready made tomato puree
¼ tsp red chilli powder, ½ tsp pepper, ¾ tsp salt or to taste, ¼ tsp sugar
½ tsp worcestershire sauce, ½ tsp soya sauce

1. Rub oil generously on a wire rack or grill of the oven.
2. Mix all ingredients of the marinade.
3. Add paneer, mushrooms and babycorns to the marinade and mix well to coat the marinade.
4. Remove from bowl and arrange on the greased wire rack or on greased wooden skewers. In the remaining marinade which is sticking to the sides of the bowl, add onion, capsicum and tomatoes. Leave these in the bowl itself. Marinate all for atleast ½ hour.
5. Grill paneer and vegetables in the oven at 180°C/410°F for 12-15 minutes or roast in a gas tandoor, spooning a little oil (basting) on them in between.
6. For the barbecue sauce - heat oil or butter in a kadhai. Add garlic and cook till light brown. Add tomatoes, tomato puree and red chilli powder and cook for 5 minutes till well blended. Add all other ingredients

and ½ cup water to get a thin sauce. Boil. Simmer for 2 minutes. Remove from fire and keep aside.

7. At serving time, heat 2 tbsp oil in a large non stick pan or a big kadhai and add the onion and capsicum. Toss for 1-2 minutes. Reduce flame.

8. Add grilled paneer, mushroom and babycorns. Keep them spread out in the pan on fire for 3-4 minutes on low heat, stirring occasionally. Add the tomatoes.

9. To serve, put some hot sauce on the serving plate. Arrange grilled vegetables on the sauce with or without skewers. Pour some hot sauce over the vegetables. Serve at once. You may serve the vegetables on rice too and serve the extra sauce in a separate sauce boat.

Note:

- When skewering delicate vegetables it is advisable to use thinner skewers, then there is less chance of the vegetable to break.
- To keep the tandoori food soft and succulent, it is important to baste the food with a little melted butter/oil or sometimes the left over marinade. To baste, just pour the oil/butter on the food that is being barbecued when it is a little more than half done.

Tandoori Paneer ki Subzi

A delightful paneer dish which is relished with meals as a side dish.

Picture on back cover   *Serves 4*

250 gms paneer - cut into 1" cubes
¾ tsp salt
¼ tsp red chilli powder
1 tsp lemon juice, 1 tbsp oil
2 capsicums - cut into fine rings
2 onions - cut into fine rings, ¼ tsp kaala namak (black salt), ¼ tsp salt
2 tsp tandoori masala
¼ tsp haldi (turmeric powder) or a pinch of tandoori red colour

GRIND TO A ROUGH PASTE WITHOUT ANY WATER
1½" piece ginger, 2-3 green chillies
1 tsp jeera (cumin seeds), 3-4 flakes garlic - optional

BASTING (POURING ON THE PANEER)
1 tbsp oil or melted butter

1. Grind garlic, ginger, jeera and green chillies to a thick rough paste. Do not add water. Keep the ginger paste aside.
2. Add salt, chilli powder and lemon juice to the paste. Add a little haldi or colour to the paste.
3. Cut paneer into 1" squares. Apply ¾ of this paste nicely on all the pieces. Keep the left over paste aside.
4. Grill this paneer on a greased wire rack and grill at 180°C for 10 minutes. Baste (pour) with melted butter or oil and grill for another 5 minutes till it is dry and slightly crisp on the outside. Keep aside till serving time.
5. At serving time, heat 1 tbsp oil in a kadhai. Fry onion and capsicum rings for a few minutes till onions turn transparent. Keep aside a few capsicum rings for garnishing.
6. Add the ginger paste and few drops of lemon juice. Add kala namak and salt.
7. Add tandoori paneer pieces. Sprinkle tandoori masala. Toss for a minutes till the paneer turns soft and is heated properly.
8. Serve immediately, garnished with the capsicum rings kept aside and garnished papad (see page 102).

Tandoori Chaat

Picture on page 85   *Serves 4*

2 capsicums - deseed & cut into 1½" pieces (preferably 1 green & 1 red capsicum)

200 gm paneer - cut into 1" cubes (8 pieces)

2 small onions - each cut into 4 pieces

4 fresh pineapple slices - each cut into 4 pieces (see note)

2 tomatoes - each cut into 4 pieces and pulp removed

1 tsp garam masala

2 tbsp lemon juice

1 tbsp tandoori masala or barbecue masala

2 tbsp oil

1 tsp salt, or to taste

1½ tsp chaat masala

1. Mix all the vegetables, pineapple and paneer in a bowl.
2. Sprinkle all the ingredients on them. Mix well.
3. Grease the grill or wire rack of the oven or tandoor and first place the paneer, pineapple and onions only on the grill rack. Grill at 180°C for about 15 minutes, till the edges start to change colour.
4. After the paneer is almost done, put the capsicum and tomatoes also on the wire rack with the paneer etc. Grill for 10 minutes.
5. Remove from the oven straight to the serving plate. Sprinkle some chaat masala and lemon juice, if you like.

Note: If tinned pineapple is being used, grill it in the second batch with capsicum and tomatoes since it is already soft.

INDIAN BREADS
Paranthas, Nans & Rotis

Tandoori Chaat : Recipe on page 82 ➤

Nan Badaami

Makes 6

2½ cups (250 gms) maida (plain flour)
½ cup hot milk
1 tsp baking powder
½ cup warm water (approx.)
½ tsp salt
6-8 badaam (almonds) - skinned & cut into long thin pieces (slivered)
1 tbsp kasoori methi (dry fenugreek leaves)

1. Heat milk and put it in a shallow bowl or a paraat. Add baking powder to the hot milk. Mix well and keep it aside for 1-2 minutes till it starts to bubble.
2. Sift maida and salt together. Add maida to the hot milk. Mix.
3. Knead to a dough with just enough warm water to get a dough of rolling consistency. Knead once again with wet hands till very smooth and elastic.

4. Keep covered with a damp cloth in a warm place for 3-4 hours.
5. Make 6-8 balls. Cover with a damp cloth and keep aside for 15 minutes.
6. Heat a gas tandoor for 10 minutes on fire.
7. Roll out each ball to an oblong shape. Spread ghee all over. Fold 1" from one side (lengthways), so as to overlap an inch of the nan. Press on the joint with the belan (rolling pin).
8. Sprinkle some blanched (skin removed by dipping in hot water) and chopped almonds and kasoori methi. Press with a rolling pin (belan) lightly. Pull one side of the nan to give it a pointed end like the shape of the nan.
9. Apply some water on the back side of the nan. Stick in a hot gas tandoor.
10. Cook till nan is ready. Spread butter on the ready nan & serve hot.

Note: You can make plain nan also with the same recipe. Just don't use badaam in the above recipe for a plain nan.

Lachha Parantha

Makes 6

2 cups atta (wheat flour), ½ tsp salt, 2 tbsp ghee, ½ cup milk, ½ cup water

1. Sift flour & salt in a paraat. Rub in 1 tbsp ghee till flour turns crumbly.
2. Mix water and milk together. Make a well in the middle of the flour. Pour milk-water mix gradually. Knead well to a dough of rolling consistency. Keep covered with a damp cloth for ½ hour.
3. Make 6 balls. Roll out each ball to a circle of 6" diameter. Spread some ghee all over. Sprinkle dry atta on half of the circle.
4. Fold into ½ & get semi-circle. Spread ghee all over. Put dry atta on ½ part semi-circle. Fold again lengthwise into ½ & you get a long strip.
5. Apply ghee all over on the strip. Roll the strip from one end till the end, to form a flattened ball (pedha). Press gently. Roll out, applying very little pressure, to form the lachha parantha. If too much pressure is applied, the layers stick to each other and do not open up later.
6. Stick in a heated tandoor or shallow fry on a tawa. Place on a clean napkin & crush the parantha slightly, to open up the layers. Serve hot.

Tandoori Roti

Makes 6-7

2½ cups atta (whole wheat flour), ½ tsp salt, 1 cup water (approx.)

PASTE TO SPREAD
2 tbsp ghee or oil mixed with 1 tbsp maida

1. Make a soft dough with atta, salt and water. Keep aside for half an hour.
2. Divide the dough into 6 equal balls. Flatten each ball, roll out each into a round of 5" diameter.
3. Spread some ghee mixed with maida.
4. Make a slit, starting from any one end till almost to the other end, leaving just 1".
5. Start rolling from the slit, to form an even cone.
6. Keeping the cone upright, press slightly to get a flattened, coiled disc.
7. Roll out with a belan to a diameter of 5", applying pressure only at the centre and not on the sides. The layers do not open if pressure is applied on the sides. Cook in a hot tandoor till brown specs appear.

Roomali Roti

Picture on page 29   *Makes 12*

DOUGH
1½ cups maida (plain flour)
1 cup atta
2 tbsp oil
½ tsp salt

PASTE
2 tbsp ghee
1 tbsp maida (plain flour)

1. Mix maida, atta, oil and salt with a little water to make a slightly stiff dough like dough for puris. Keep aside covered with a damp cloth for 1 hour.
2. Make a paste of ghee and maida in a small bowl.
3. Make 2 lemon sized balls of the dough.

4. Roll out 1 ball to the size of a puri, about 5-6" diameter.
5. Spread 1 tsp of the ghee-maida paste on it. Keep aside in a plate.
6. Roll the second ball to the same size again and put this on the first roti spread with ghee.
7. Place the sandwiched rotis on the chakla and roll out together to a large thin roti using a little dry flour for rolling.
8. Heat a tawa on low heat and cook this roti on both sides very quickly. Do not make it brown.
9. Remove from fire and immediately separate the 2 rotis stuck by the paste.
10. Fold each roti into a triangle and keep soft in a casserole.

Chutneys & Salads

Dahi Poodina Chutney

Serves 6

GRIND TOGETHER

½ cup poodina (mint), ½ cup hara dhania (green coriander)
2 green chillies
½ onion, 2 flakes garlic
a pinch of kala namak, ¼ tsp bhuna jeera, salt to taste

ADD LATER

1½ cups curd - hang for 15 minutes
1 tsp oil

1. Wash coriander and mint leaves.
2. Grind coriander, mint, green chillies, onion and garlic with a little water to a paste.
3. Beat curd well till smooth.
4. To the hung curd, add the green paste, oil, kala namak, bhuna jeera and salt to taste. Serve with tandoori food.

Chil li Garlic Chutney

Serves 8

4-5 dry red chillies - deseeded and soaked in ¼ cup water
6-8 flakes garlic, 1 tsp saboot dhania, 1 tsp jeera, 1 tbsp oil
½ tsp salt, 1 tsp sugar, 3 tbsp vinegar, ½ tsp soya sauce

1. For the chutney, grind the soaked chillies along with the water, garlic, dhania, jeera, oil and sugar and vinegar to a paste. Add soya sauce.

Poodina Chutney

Serves 6

½ cup poodina leaves (½ bunch)
1 cup hara dhania (coriander) - chopped along with the stem
2 green chillies - chopped, 1 onion - chopped
1½ tsp amchoor (dried mango powder), 1½ tsp sugar, ½ tsp salt

1. Wash coriander and mint leaves.
2. Grind all ingredients with just enough water to get the right chutney consistency.

Sirke Waale Pyaaz

Serves 4-6

13 small onions, ½ cup vinegar, ½ cup water, 1 tsp salt, ½ tsp chilli powder

1. Peel onions. Make a cross slit on each onion on the top.
2. Place in a bowl. Sprinkle salt and chilli powder on them and rub well.
3. Boil water and vinegar together in a pan. Remove from fire.
4. Pour the hot vinegar water over the onions in the bowl.
5. When the vinegar cools a little, transfer the onions and vinegar into a clean bottle. Keep in the refrigerator. Use after a day.

Note: A few ginger match sticks and green chillies can also be added.

Peanut Cabbage Relish

Here is a totally different way of using peanuts. This relish goes well with almost all tandoori recipes.

Serves 6

6 tbsp roasted peanuts - crushed coarsely
1 small cabbage - chopped very finely
1 tbsp green coriander - minced
2 green chillies - minced
juice of 2 lemons, or to taste
2 tsp sugar
1 tsp salt, or to taste

1. Mix ½ tsp salt in the cabbage and set aside for 10 minutes to sweat.
2. Coarsely crush the peanuts on a chakla-belan (rolling board and pin).
3. Put peanuts in a bowl. Add all other ingredients except the cabbage.
4. Squeeze the cabbage. Mix well and serve.

ACCOMPANIMENTS

Some favourites to make the meal complete with the kebabs

Dal Makhani

Picture on page 29　　　　　*Serves 6*

1 cup urad saboot (whole black beans)
2 tbsp channe ki dal (split gram dal)
1 tbsp ghee or oil
5 cups of water, 1½ tsp salt
3 tbsp ghee or oil
5 large tomatoes - pureed in a grinder
2 tsp dhania powder (coriander), ½ tsp garam masala
1 tbsp kasoori methi (dry fenugreek leaves)
2 tsp tomato ketchup
2-3 tbsp butter, ½ cup milk, ½ cup cream
a pinch of jaiphal (nutmeg)

GRIND TO A PASTE

2 dry whole red chillies, preferably Kashmiri red chillies - deseeded & soaked
for 10 minutes and then drained, 1" piece ginger, 5-6 flakes garlic

1. Pressure cook both dals with 5 cups water, 1 tbsp ghee, salt and the ginger-garlic-chilli paste.
2. After the first whistle, keep on low flame for 40 minutes. Remove from fire. After the pressure drops, mash the hot dal a little. Keep aside.
3. Heat ghee. Add tomatoes pureed in a grinder. Cook until thick & dry.
4. Add the garam masala & coriander powder. Cook until ghee separates.
5. Add kasoori methi. Cook further for 1-2 minutes.
6. Add this tomato mixture to the boiled dal.
   Add tomato ketchup.
7. Add butter. Simmer on low flame for 20-25 minutes, stirring & mashing the dal occasionally with a karchhi against the sides of the cooker.
8. Add milk. Mix very well with a karchhi. Simmer for 15-20 minutes more, to get the right colour and smoothness.
9. Reduce heat. Add jaiphal. Mix. Add cream gradually, stirring continuously. Remove from fire. Serve.

Note: Originally the dal was cooked by leaving it overnight on the burning coal angithis. The longer the dal simmered, the better it tasted.

Paneer Makhani

Serves 4

250 gm paneer - cut into 1" cubes
5 large (500 gm) tomatoes - each cut into 4 pieces
2 tbsp desi ghee or butter and 2 tbsp oil
½ tsp jeera (cumin seeds)
4-5 flakes garlic and 1" piece ginger - ground to a paste (1½ tsp ginger-garlic paste)
1 tbsp kasoori methi (dried fenugreek leaves), 1 tsp tomato ketchup
2 tsp dhania powder, ½ tsp garam masala, 1 tsp salt, or to taste
½ tsp red chilli powder, preferably degi mirch, ½ cup water
½-1 cup milk, approx., ½ cup cream (optional)

CASHEW PASTE (KAJU PASTE)

3 tbsp cashewnuts - soaked in ¼ cup warm water for 15 minutes and ground to a very fine paste

1. Boil tomatoes in ½ cup water. Simmer for 4-5 minutes on low heat till tomatoes turn soft. Remove from fire and cool. Grind the tomatoes along with the water to a smooth puree.

2. Heat oil and ghee or butter in a kadhai. Reduce heat. Add jeera. When it turns golden, add ginger-garlic paste.
3. When paste starts to change colour add the above tomato puree and cook till absolutely dry.
4. Add kasoori methi and tomato ketchup.
5. Add masalas - dhania powder, garam masala, salt and red chilli powder. Mix well for a few seconds. Cook till oil separates.
6. Add cashew paste. Mix well for 2 minutes.
7. Add water. Boil. Simmer on low heat for 4-5 minutes. Reduce heat.
8. Add the paneer cubes. Keep aside to cool till serving time.
9. At serving time, add enough milk to the cold paneer masala to get a thick curry, mix gently. (Remember to add milk only after the masala turns cold, to prevent the milk from curdling. After adding milk, heat curry on low heat.)
10. Heat on low heat, stirring continuously till just about to boil.
11. Add cream, keeping the heat very low and stirring continuously. Remove from fire immediately.
12. Garnish with 1 tbsp fresh cream, slit green chillies and coriander.

Garnished Papad

Serves 12

15 mini papads
1 onion - chopped, 2-3 green chillies - chopped
2 tbsp chopped coriander, 1 tbsp butter or oil
2 tbsp freshly grated coconut (optional)
1 tomato - deseeded and cut into tiny pieces (diced)
¼ tsp red chilli powder, ½ tsp salt or to taste, ¼ tsp pepper
2 tbsp ready-made bikaneri bhujiya or aloo bhujiya (optional)

1. Heat 1 tbsp butter or oil.
2. Add onion & green chillies. Cook till soft. Add chopped fresh coriander, red chilli powder, salt, pepper and freshly shredded coconut. Mix well. Cook for 3-4 minutes. Add tomatoes. Mix and remove from fire.
3. Roast or fry mini papads. Spread spoon full of mixture on each papad.
4. Sprinkle some bhujiya (about ½ tsp) & chaat masala on each papad.
5. Serve with poodina chutney (see page 94).

Hare Chholia Ke Kebab : Recipe on page 69 ➤